Introduction

The English Electric 2700 hp class 50 locomotives were introduced in 1967 and at first worked on the LMR, particularly on the West Coast route. In the early 1970s they were used in pairs on Anglo-Scottish services between Crewe and Glasgow while the main line was being electrified. As the need for their services on the LMR diminished after 1974, they were gradually transferred to the Western Region and by 1976 the whole class was allocated to the WR.

On the WR they were intended to replace the diesel-hydraulic 'Westerns', which were being phased out and withdrawn, but it took some time for their reliability and availability to improve sufficiently to dispense completely with the hydraulics. It was really only after the decision to carry out a mid-life refurbishment programme, commencing with No. 50006 in 1979, that the class began to give of their best. The refurbishment programme, together with the addition of a series of fine-sounding naval names and the adoption of a more colourful livery in place of the former plain BR blue, took the locomotives into the 1980s in fine style.

By this time, however, further changes in motive power policy had taken place and many WR passenger services were being worked by Inter-City 125 High-Speed Trains. Once again the 50s found themselves taking on new duties, this time on the former Southern Region West of England route from Waterloo to Exeter.

Withdrawals began in 1987 and on present plans should be completed by 1991. But the 50s, or 'Hoovers' as they are affectionately known, are a very popular class amongst enthusiasts and their supporters are already raising funds to secure one or more locomotives [...] impressive machine[...] it has been for the [...]

This book fea[...] Devon and Cornwall, w[...] what better setting in which to see these powerful locomotives than on the railways of Devon and Cornwall, an area which has an abundance of photogenic locations and, until recently, was very rich in semaphore signalling.

The railways of Devon have an atmosphere of their own, especially where the main line runs alongside the popular South Devon coast, before skirting the fringes of the beautiful but brooding Dartmoor. Cornwall, reached after crossing Brunel's famous Saltash Bridge, has more viaducts than the Settle to Carlisle route and still has a few fine GWR stations.

In writing and compiling this book I would like to thank the following people for all their help: The railwaymen of the Western Region, especially Michael James of Laira Traction and Maintenance Depot at Plymouth; to the farmers and landowners of the two counties for permission to 'trespass' on their land in order to obtain that elusive picture; to Martin Beckett, Geoff Gillham, Tom Heavyside, Les Nixon and Graham Roose for use of their photographs; to Joan Wappett for sterling work at the typewriter and my wife Christina for helping with the layout and that valuable second opinion. Lastly to my publisher Roger Hardingham. *Note.* Unless stated all pictures were taken by the author.

Roger Siviter ARPS

©Roger Siviter &
Kingfisher Railway Productions
ISBN 0 946184 51 8
1989

Typeset by
Alphaset
65A The Avenue
Southampton

Printed by
The Amadeus Press
Huddersfield
Yorkshire

Above: What better way to start an appreciation of the class 50s. A pair, Nos. 50018 *Resolution* and 50044 *Exeter*, head the 1024 Penzance – Birmingham New Street service through Bodmin on 30th May 1984.

Front cover: The impressive Clinnick viaduct in Cornwall takes the strain as No. 50027 *Lion* crosses with the 1505 Plymouth – Penzance on 29th May 1985. *Christina Siviter*

Back cover: No. 50149 near Ivybridge with the 1455 St. Blazey – Gloucester goods. 8th April 1988.

Published by

Kingfisher Railway Productions

65A The Avenue, Southampton SO1 2TA

No. 50030 *Repulse* hurries out of Whiteball Tunnel with a morning relief Birmingham New Street – Paignton train on 5th April 1985. Despite using full power on the climb up from Wellington, speed will have been dropping steadily but will soon be regained on the descent towards Exeter. Whiteball marks the county boundaries of Devon and Somerset. The signalbox here dates from the 1950s, the earlier one having been burnt out. The box, semaphores and 'down' refuge sidings have all now been removed.

Opposite page top: When this picture was taken on 7th May 1985, Tiverton Junction still boasted an impressive array of semaphores. Framed by a variety of these signals is No. 50002 *Superb* as it approaches the station with 1S71, the 0730 Penzance – Glasgow & Edinburgh train which it will work as far as Birmingham. This station has since been closed and a new one built at Tiverton Parkway some three miles east, close to the site of the former station of Sampford Peverell.

Opposite page bottom: An 'up' ECS train hauled by No. 50030 climbs the steep grade to Whiteball tunnel on 6th April 1985. The location is Burlescombe. The impressive looking locomotives with their 16 cylinders and four exhaust ports make a tremendous sound when working against the grade.

Above: With the mid-summer sun almost overhead, unrefurbished No. 50002 brings the lightly loaded 0830 Paddington – St. Austell car carrier through Dawlish Warren on Sunday 20th June 1982. *G.F. Gillham*

Right: No. 50032 *Courageous* is seen reversing the 'up' car carrier train into Newton Abbot station on Saturday 7th July 1984. Prior to 1982 passenger coaches were attached to this train thus forming a complete motorail train, but from that year onwards passengers travelled by normal service train. This service has now been discontinued and major reconstruction at Newton Abbot has reduced the facilities to three platforms. It was very rare by 1984 to find class 50s on this service, the usual motive power being class 47s.

Opposite page top: No. 50017 *Royal Oak* is seen at Cockwood Harbour near Starcross on the evening of 12th April 1983 with an 'up' freight. This locomotive was one of the first six to be refurbished and hence still carries the BR plain blue livery. The later 'large logo' livery was first applied to the class in 1980 with No. 50023.

Opposite page bottom: Langstone Rock dominates the background of this picture of No. 50022 *Anson* as it approaches Dawlish Warren on 31st October 1984 with the 1050 Totnes – Waterloo train.

A lowly task for No. 50007 as it approaches Newton Abbot with a 'down' evening hopper train on 23rd April 1987.

No. 50044 *Exeter* approaches Totnes with a 'down' ballast train on 29th May 1984. Of note are the installed, but not commissioned, colour light signal posts for the 'up' line.

Skirting the edge of Dartmoor on 13th April 1988 is No. 50004 *St Vincent* with an air-braked freight from St. Blazey yard. The location is Dinnaton just west of Ivybridge. The distinctive white china clay spoil heaps in the background give a clue to the nature of this freight train, for the leading CargoWagon and the three PolyBulks behind it have originated in the Cornish clay district.

Above: Immediately on leaving Exeter St Davids trains bound for Waterloo are faced with a steep climb of 1 in 37 up to Exeter Central station. On 11th April 1983 No. 50033 *Glorious* is seen descending the bank from Central with an afternoon train from Waterloo. Exeter St Davids West signalbox, now vanished, was of wooden construction and also worthy of note is the GWR-type semaphore signal complete with route indicator. Class 33 No. 33026 is stabled on the left.

Left: Semaphore signals are in abundance in this view of No. 50046 *Ajax* in charge of the 1130 New Street – Penzance train as it approaches Dawlish Warren on a misty 1st November 1984.

Opposite page top: This picture was taken at the site of Hele and Bradninch station on 7th May 1985. It shows pannier tank No. 1638 *Dartington* (introduced by the Western Region in 1949 but to a GWR design) in the siding at the former station while in the background is No. 50011 *Centurion* hurrying past with the 1445 Paddington – Penzance train.

Opposite page bottom: No. 50049 *Defiance* pounds through Totnes on Sunday 19th August 1984 with the 1045 Paddington – Penzance train, normally an HST service. Note the GWR signalbox and hanging flower baskets on the station canopy as well as the porters' trollies.

Above: A glorious sight for class 50 enthusiasts as No. 50011 *Centurion* charges up Rattery bank on a beautiful late spring evening with the 0923 Newcastle – Penzance train on 28th May 1985. The exact location is Ashridge some half a mile to the east of Tigley. The steepest grade here is 1 in 46.

Opposite page top: No. 50024 in the revised Network South-East livery, which dates from August 1987, is seen just east of Ivybridge in charge of a 'down' evening train of permanent way materials, mainly new concrete sleepers. *Vanguard* is one of a few 50s to carry miniature snow ploughs which it seems to retain throughout the year. Strangely, they appear on one end only. 13th April 1988.

Opposite page bottom: No. 50007 has just passed Aller Junction and heads for Newton Abbot with the 1745 Paignton – Paddington train on 7th July 1984. The line from Plymouth, which marks the foot of Dainton Bank, is clearly seen coming in from the right.

Above: Framed by the impressive signal gantry which used to adorn the western end of Newton Abbot station is No. 50027 *Lion* in charge of the 0924 Paignton – New Street train on 7th September 1985.

Opposite page top: On 26th April 1984 No. 50035 *Ark Royal* is about to depart from Platform 3 at Exeter St Davids station with the 1220 service to Waterloo. The 172½ mile journey will be completed in about 3½ hours with some 15 intermediate stops. London-bound HST services on the ex-GW route depart in the opposite direction and take roughly an hour less to reach their destination.

Opposite page bottom: A few days before the semaphore signals disappeared in the Newton Abbot area we see No. 50010 *Monarch* on a morning 'up' goods framed in the fine gantry at Aller Junction on 24th April 1987. Note the old style number D410 above the cab.

Top: A vintage view on Dainton bank near Stoneycombe with No. 50003 (then unnamed, now named *Temeraire*) in charge of the 1530 Paddington – Penzance service on 8th July 1974.   *G.F. Gillham*

Above: No. 50037 *Illustrious* hammers up Dainton bank with the 0918 Penzance – Leeds on 6th April 1985. The location is Wrigwell Hill a few hundred yards before the summit. Since leaving Totnes, some five miles to the southwest, the locomotive will have worked hard against the grade for most of the time. In fact the train could be heard long before it came into view, a most exciting sound on a beautiful spring day.

Opposite page top: Another St Davids view, this time at the east end and taken on 25th April 1983. No. 50019 *Ramillies* has just arrived with the 1310 from Waterloo. Being one of the first six locomotives to be refurbished (note the central headlamp) it is still in the older livery.   *Tom Heavyside*

Opposite page bottom: No. 50027 *Lion* coasts down Honiton bank with the 1210 Exeter – Waterloo train on 19th February 1985. The location is near Wilmington where the A35 road to Bridport crosses the line.

No. 50030 *Repulse* skirts the Teign at Shaldon Bridge with the 1145 Paignton–Paddington on 8th April 1985. Note the very neat sea wall retaining the running lines.

Opposite page top: Exeter St Davids on the evening of 30th October 1984. No. 50010 *Monarch* (left) is waiting to leave with the 1934 to Waterloo while No. 50012 *Benbow* has just arrived with the 1645 Paddington–Plymouth train which is normally an HST service.

Opposite page bottom: An immaculate No. 50002 *Superb* waits at Newton Abbot with the Fridays only 1750 Paddington–Plymouth service on 18th September 1981.

G.F. Gillham

Above: A long lens accents the curves at Dawlish as No. 50049 *Defiance* races along with an 'up' midday relief train on a misty 8th July 1984. This section of line has since been resignalled for two-way operation, in the event of damage by the sea.

Opposite page top: The famous sea wall at Teignmouth is the location for No. 50011 (later named *Centurion*) in charge of a Paddington train on 6th September 1975. This locomotive was the first 50 to be withdrawn, but still exists at Crewe Works as a test bed for overhauled power units.

Les Nixon

Opposite page bottom: Another equally notable location – Horse Cove between Teignmouth and Dawlish. On 15th August 1987 No. 50048 is seen with the 1045 New Street – Paignton service.

Above: The famous junction at Cowley Bridge (one mile to the north of Exeter St Davids station) is the setting for our next picture which shows No. 50010 *Monarch* heading the 1145 Paddington–Penzance service on Sunday 8th July 1984. The line to the left is the former Southern Railway route from Exeter to Plymouth which now terminates at Meldon Quarry, the line to Barnstaple branching off at Coleford Junction. Alas now the box and signals have all gone.

Opposite page top: Storm clouds gather as No. 50033 *Glorious* winds its way out of Exeter Central station and approaches the former SR signalbox on the first leg of its 172½ mile journey to Waterloo on 28th August 1984.

Opposite page bottom: No. 50047 *Swiftsure*, still in the old livery, approaches Exeter on 11th April 1983 with a local train from Paignton. Note the fine GWR signalbox of wooden construction and the handsome bracket signal, which denotes that the train is routed into Platform 5 at St Davids.

Above: Totnes station on 19th August 1984 witnesses No. 50036 *Victorious* with the 0945 Paddington – Plymouth about to start the stiff climb up Rattery bank.

Opposite page top: Nicely framed by the signal gantry at the eastern and of Newton Abbot station is No. 50009 in the early stages of its run from Paignton – Birmingham New Street on the 18th August 1984.

Opposite page bottom: The classic shot at Teignmouth since steam days. No. 50007 *Sir Edward Elgar* makes an impressive sight whilst turning towards the sea – side resort's beach on 16th August 1987.

Above: No. 50047 *Swiftsure* rushes through the suburbs of Plymouth with the 1500 Plymouth – Penzance on a very wet 3rd April 1985. The location is Devonport station.

Right: A wet night at Plymouth North Road station as No. 50018 obligingly poses for the camera. 2nd April 1985.

Opposite page top: No. 50006 *Neptune* (now withdrawn) approaches the popular resort of Paignton with the 1115 from Paddington on 1st September 1984.

Opposite page bottom: The River Plym provides an attractive backcloth for No. 50029 *Renown* as it approaches Plymouth Laira with the 1340 Paddington – Penzance on 28th May 1985. Laira, of course, is these days the diesel maintenance depot. In steam days, when it was home to so many famous locomotives, its code number was 83D, later 84A. Laira was once the junction for the line to Plymouth Friary (SR); this line now only leads to a goods yard about a mile distant, along which is situated the carriage washing plant etc.

No. 50042 *Triumph* pulls through the now closed station at Okehampton (on the former Southern route to Plymouth) with a ballast train from Meldon Quarry. There have been occasional DMU services to and from Exeter on summer weekends in recent years. *Graham Roose*

This general view inside the maintenance depot at Plymouth Laira depot on 3rd April 1985 shows a number of class 50s undergoing a variety of work. No. 50029 is on the lefthand side of the picture and behind it is No. 50028 *Tiger*.

Liskeard viaduct is the attractive setting for our next picture and shows No. 50013 *Agincourt* heading eastwards with the five-coach 1135 Penzance – Plymouth local train. This train stops at all stations on this route except those between Saltash and Plymouth North Road where it arrives at 1341. Liskeard station is just on the left-hand side of the picture, while out of sight below the viaduct runs the Liskeard – Looe branch.

No. 50047 *Swiftsure* (now withdrawn) crosses Gover viaduct near St Austell with the 0740 Penzance – New Street service on 1st August 1983.

Les Nixon

The 0940 Paddington – Penzance train with No. 50020 *Revenge* in charge enters Liskeard station on 29th May 1985. Note the loop line which serves the platform for the Looe branch. Also of interest is the GWR inverted bracket signal on the 'up' platform.

The delightful station at St Austell is the setting as No. 50017 *Royal Oak* waits to leave with the mid-day Penzance – Plymouth parcels train on 27th April 1984. The sidings and platform on the right were, until recent years, used by the motorail trains, St Austell being the terminus for these trains.

Above: No. 50149 *Defiance* (formerly No. 50049) now resplendent in Rail Freight livery which it received in Autumn 1987 is seen crossing the causeway at Golant on the Fowey branch with Carne Point – Par china clay empties. April 1988. Note the new CDA wagons, the old 'hood' wagons having been withdrawn some months earlier. The main modification required for Rail Freight service of No. 50149 was the use of re-geared bogies similar to those used on the class 37s. The conversion reflected an attempt to get more useful work out of the class 50s in their declining years as the need for them on passenger trains decreased. In the event, *Defiance* was the only one to be so modified and even this proved to be of short duration, the loco being restored to normal specification early in 1989.

Les Nixon

Opposite page: Bodmin Parkway station (formerly Bodmin Road) still boasts a very fine GWR footbridge, although the semaphore signals have disappeared. The signalbox still exists on the 'down' platform where it is now used as the station buffet – run by an enthusiast! No. 50026 *Indomitable* growls its way out of the station on 1st June 1985 with the 0740 Penzance – Glasgow service. Bodmin Parkway is the junction for the line to Wenford Bridge via Bodmin General and Boscarne Junction. Originally this line was GWR to Boscarne Junction where it met the LSWR line from Wadebridge to Wenford Bridge, trains from Bodmin to Wenford Bridge needing the reverse at Boscarne Junction. Until quite recently this line was still being used for freight traffic (china clay) but this has now stopped. However, this famous line is now preserved including the beautiful GWR station at Bodmin which is still in very good order.

The lovely old GWR platform buildings have now gone from Lostwithiel station but the splendid signalbox and many GWR type semaphore signals still remain. No. 50017 rattles over the crossing and enters the station on 31st May 1985 with the 1505 Plymouth – Penzance local train.

Our next location is at St Dennis Junction on the Newquay branch and the train, hauled by No. 50034, is the 1900 (Saturdays only) Par – Newquay service. The line diverging to the right once ran through to Burngullow (on the Plymouth – Penzance line) and also served the branch to Meledor Mill. There are proposals to restore the St Dennis Junction – Burngullow line and re-route Newquay services via St Austell rather than Par. The signalbox and passing loop have now disappeared from this scene.

On the 22nd August 1987 No. 50034 *Furious* leaves the Newquay branch and enters Par station with the 1628 Newquay–Wolverhampton service. St Blazey shed and yard is situated off the Newquay branch half a mile or so from Par station.

On a late spring evening No. 50017 is framed by a GWR type semaphore signal and a fine example of a GWR signalbox as it enters Truro station with the 0922 Newcastle–Penzance train on 30th May 1984. The cathedral city of Truro still has a very fine station complete with GWR style buildings and footbridges.

Left: The station at Truro is in sight for the passengers of the 0823 Plymouth – Penzance local service on 30th May 1985. This train started from Exeter at 0700, calling at all stations (except Dawlish Warren) on its way to Plymouth. The train, hauled by No. 50050 *Fearless*, is seen crossing the graceful Carvedras viaduct. Truro boasts two viaducts, the other being Truro just to the east of here. The church dominating the scene is St George The Martyr, and at the foot of the viaduct is part of the Victoria Gardens.

Below: No. 50030 *Repulse* powers the 0932 Penzance – Paddington train across Derrycombe viaduct on Saturday 1st June 1985. The gradient here is 1 in 70. Between Liskeard and Bodmin Parkway there are nine major viaducts in just nine miles. The line here threads through the Glynn Valley which is part of the Fowey Valley. The viaduct is situated three miles to the east of Bodmin Parkway station.

No. 50047 once again, this time bringing a 'down' load of flat wagons across Liskeard viaduct on the morning of 27th August 1987.

No. 50149 *Defiance* is seen with a short goods train leaving the Parkandillack branch at Burngullow and heading for St Austell on 6th April 1988. As an economy measure the main line from Burngullow to Probus has been singled.

A view taken from the new Hayle bypass on 6th May 1988 and showing No. 50032 *Courageous* soon after leaving St Erth with the 1213 Penzance – Plymouth local train. Most of these local services are now in the hands of class 155 Sprinters. *Courageous* is the only member of the class to have its nameplate with a blue rather than red background.

First built, though highest numbered, No. 50050 *Fearless* has just crossed over Tregagne viaduct with the 1115 Penzance – Plymouth local train on 30th May 1985. A short distance away to the west of here is Tregeagle viaduct. The small stream which Tregagne viaduct crosses runs into the River Tresillian which eventually runs into the River Fal just north of Falmouth.

Emerging from Treverrin tunnel (565 yards long) on 31st May 1985 is No. 50023 with the 1635 Plymouth – Penzance. Treverrin tunnel gave its builders many problems in the last century being a very wet and damp structure requiring special drainage precautions. This stretch of line was doubled in 1894.

St Erth change for St Ives. No. 50026 *Indomitable* hauls a 'down' special from the North of England to Penzance on 30th May 1985 into St Erth. This scene reflects one which is not dissimilar to the one when steam was present. The branch to St Ives curls away to the left.

No. 50043 *Eagle* takes the Fowey branch at Lostwithiel with a string of the old china clay 'hood' wagons on 23rd April 1987. The main line behind the train climbs steeply towards Treverrin tunnel.   *Les Nixon*

Shunting china clay wagons at Parkandillack clay works on 24th April 1987 is No. 50047. The line to Parkandillack runs from Burngullow Junction situated to the west of St Austell.   *Les Nixon*

No. 50023 *Howe* crosses Moorswater viaduct on 5th April 1988 with the 0910 Plymouth – Penzance service. The stone piers for the old timber viaduct can be clearly seen. The Liskeard and Caradon Railway ran beneath, closing in 1917.

Crossing the graceful Coombe St Stephen viaduct on the evening of 29th May 1985 is No. 50010 *Monarch* with the 1340 Paddington – Penzance train.

Rounding the curves of Buckshead (east of Truro) is No. 50012 *Benbow* with the 1557 Plymouth – Penzance service on 5th April 1988. This view demonstrates well the extreme curvatures on Cornwall's main line.

No. 50033 *Glorious* has just left Buckshead tunnel and is heading towards Probus and St Austell with the 1525 Penzance – Plymouth service on 5th April 1988.

An easy task for No. 50019 *Ramillies* on 13th September 1982 as it slows the 1350 Plymouth – Penzance local for the stop at Lostwithiel.*G.F. Gillham*

No. 50016 *Barham* looks a splendid sight as it rushes through the site of the old station at Marazion and past some very famous landmarks – the Pullman car camping coaches – with the 1024 Penzance – Liverpool service on 17th August 1984. The 50s really make a terrific sound when they are working hard and this one was heard all the way from Penzance, two miles away. The station at Marazion, along with several other stations in Cornwall, was closed in October 1964. The camping coaches have since been given a new lease of life.

Above: A glorious summer morning at Penzance as No. 50005 *Collingwood* prepares to leave with the 0932 Penzance – Paddington train, one of the great train journeys of the British Isles. The train will take just under six hours to complete the 305¼ miles to Paddington. The date of this picture 17th August 1984. The sleeper from Paddington stands in Platform 1.

Opposite page top: No. 50044 *Exeter* pulls away from Penzance station with the mid-day parcels train bound for Plymouth and the north on 29th August 1984. The main line is single track from Penzance to just west of Marazion, the other two tracks being for ECS movements. The middle track was the normal 'up' line.

Opposite page bottom: A busy scene at Penzance on the evening of 5th May 1988. No. 50016 *Barham* is about to bring extra carriages into the station to form the 1830 to Bristol. No. 50036 *Victorious* is seen at the head of the 1922 'up' postal train. This train no longer runs as depicted, but now runs to the north with only three vans.